Alcatraz
Indian Land Forever

Troy Johnson has conducted extensive research into the occupation of Alcatraz Island and subsequent American Indian activism. He holds a master's degree in American Indian history and law and a Ph.D. in U.S. history from the University of California, Los Angeles, where he currently is a research scholar in the American Indian Studies Center.

———————

The American Indian Studies Center at the University of California, Los Angeles was founded in 1969 and ranks among the top research centers of its kind in the country. The Center serves the educational and cultural needs of the University's American Indian community, including faculty, staff, resident scholars, researchers, undergraduate and graduate students. The Center sponsors national conferences, workshops, lectures, and symposia and a pre- and postdoctoral fellowship program. The publications unit of the Center produces books, bibliographies, and monographs as well as the *American Indian Culture and Research Journal*, an internationally recognized quarterly academic journal.

For information regarding the American Indian Studies Center, to request a publications catalogue, or to order additional copies of this book, please contact the American Indian Studies Center at 3220 Campbell Hall, 405 Hilgard Avenue, University of California, Los Angeles, 90024-1548, or call (310) 825-7315.

ALCATRAZ
INDIAN LAND FOREVER

Edited by Troy R. Johnson

American Indian Studies Center
University of California
405 Hilgard Avenue
Los Angeles, California 90024-1548

Editor: Troy R. Johnson, American Indian Studies Center, UCLA
Publications Editor: Duane Champagne, Sociology Department, UCLA
Managing Editor: Judith St. George, American Indian Studies Center, UCLA
Photography Editor: Stephen Lehmer, Art Department, UCLA

ACKNOWLEDGMENTS

Portions of the material in this collection have been published previously in *Alcatraz Is Not an Island: Indians of All Tribes* (Berkeley, CA: Wingbow Press, 1972); *Mankiller: A Chief and Her People* by Wilma Mankiller and Michael Wallis (New York: St. Martin's Press, 1993); *Seeds of Change* by Herman J. Viola and Carolyn Margolis (Washington, DC: Smithsonian Press, 1991); *Behind the Trail of Broken Treaties: An Indian Declaration of Independence* by Vine Deloria, Jr. (New York: Delacorte Press, 1974); *California History; New York Times Magazine; Parade; Indian Voice; Ramparts;* and *Akwesasne Notes.*

Special thanks to Research Archives, San Francisco History Room, San Francisco Public Library; Doris Duke Oral History Project, Salt Lake City, Utah; American Indian Historical Research Project, University of New Mexico, Albuquerque; United States Department of the Interior, National Park Service (John Noxon and Deborah Marcus, photographers). Quotes from "Radio Free Alcatraz" are printed with the permission of Pacifica Radio Archive, North Hollywood, California.

Printed by Edwards Brothers Incorporated

American Indian Studies Center
University of California
405 Hilgard Avenue
Los Angeles, California 90024-1548
USA

On November 9, 1969, a group of American Indian college students and urban Indian people from the San Francisco Bay area set out in a chartered boat, the *Monte Cristo*, to circle Alcatraz Island and symbolically claim the island for Indian people. On November 20, 1969, this symbolic occupation of Alcatraz Island turned into a full-scale occupation when Indian students from San Francisco State University, the University of California, Berkeley, the University of California, Santa Cruz, and the University of California, Los Angeles, joined with urban Indian people from the greater San Francisco Bay area and reoccupied the island, claiming title by "right of discovery." Various Indian occupiers held the island until June 11, 1971, focusing the attention of the American people on the treatment of the first Americans. In a statement to the Congress of the United States, President Richard Nixon categorized this treatment as follows:

> The first Americans—the Indians—are the most deprived and most isolated minority group in our nation. On virtually every scale of measurement—employment, income, education, health—the condition of the Indian people ranks at the bottom.

The newly formed Alcatraz organization, Indians of All Tribes, Inc., kept Americans aware of the occupation and their demands by publishing a newsletter, *Rock Talk* and by starting their own radio program "Radio Free Alcatraz," which was broadcast in Berkeley on radio station KPFA, in Los Angeles on KPFK, and in New York City on WBAI. As a result, letters and telegrams began to pour in to government officials, including the president. The mood of the public could be summed up in a telegram sent to President Nixon on November 26, 1969 that read, "For once in this country's history let the Indians have something. Let them have Alcatraz."

Alcatraz soon became a rallying cry for the new American Indian activism that would continue into the mid-1970s under the names of Red Power and the American Indian Movement. This activism included the 1972 occupation of the Bureau of Indian Affairs headquarters in Washington, D.C, which lasted for seven days, and the occupation of Wounded Knee II in 1973, which lasted for seventy-one days.

The occupation of Alcatraz Island remains a poorly documented event, even though it represents the longest continuous occupation of a federal facility by any minority group in the history of this nation. Yet it is on Alcatraz that modern activism finds its roots. Alcatraz set in motion a wave of overtly nationalist Indian militancy that ultimately resulted in abandonment of the U.S. government's policy of termination and the adoption of a policy of Indian self-determination. Another result was the return of the sacred Taos Blue Lake and 48,000 acres of land to the Taos Indians. In addition, 40 million acres of land were returned to the Navajo, 21,000 acres of Mount Adams in Washington State were returned to the Yakima tribe, eighty acres to the Washoe tribe in California in October 1970, and some 60,000 acres to the Warm Springs tribes of Oregon.

Today Alcatraz Island remains a strong symbol of Indian activism and self-determination, and a rallying point for unified Indian political activities. On February 11, 1978, Indian participants began the "Longest Walk" to Washington, D.C. to protest the government's ill treatment of Indian people. That walk began on Alcatraz Island. On February 11, 1994, AIM leaders Dennis Banks, Clyde Bellecourt, and Mary Wilson met with Indian people to begin the nationwide "Walk for Justice." That walk began on Alcatraz Island. On Thanksgiving Day of each year since 1969, Indian people have gathered on Alcatraz Island to honor those who participated in the occupation and those who share in the continuing struggle for Indian self-determination. The 1969 occupation of Alcatraz Island stands out as the most symbolic, the most significant, the most successful Indian protest action of the modern era.

This publication commemorating the twenty-fifth anniversary of the Alcatraz occupation presents poetry and political statements written by Indian people during the occupation or commemorating the event. The words and the photographs presented here—most of which are being published for the first time—capture the passion of the movement as spoken and written by those most intimately involved in it. This book is a tribute to the activists who withstood the hardships of Alcatraz Island in order to build a better life for all American Indian people.

Troy R. Johnson
Editor

For Richard and Yvonne Oakes

INDIAN PROCLAMATION

To the government of the United States from Alcatraz Island, Indian Territory.

We native peoples of North America have gathered here to claim our traditional and natural right to create a meaningful use for our Great Spirit's land. Therefore let it be known that our stand for self-determination is on Alcatraz. We invite the United States to acknowledge the justice of our claim. The choice now lies with the leaders of the American Government — to use violence upon us as before to remove us from our Great Spirit's land, or to institute a real change in its dealings with the American Indian. We do not fear your threat to charge us with crimes on our land. We and all other oppressed peoples would welcome this spectacle of proof before the world of your title by genocide. Nevertheless, we seek peace . . . .

—Richard Oakes

WELCOME TO THE PEOPLE

From the West
Into the city
     Comes the Buffalo!

From the North
Into the city
     Comes the big Brown Bear!

From the East
Into the city
     Flies the Eagle low!

From the South
Into the city
     Comes the running Deer!

O, Spirit of the winds
Blow the long sweetgrass—
Stay with us in the city
Until this day is passed.

When Cheyenne, Paiute and Navajo
Greet Shoshone, Iroquois, and Sioux
Tlingit, Sac and Fox and Crow
Kiowa, Blackfeet, and Hopi, too,
Nez Percé, Seminole, and Cree
Chippewa, Mohawk, Apache!

For the spirit of the Buffalo
The Eagle and the Deer
Have come into the city
Have brought the People here!

—Lonewolf, Blackfoot

Photograph of Geronimo, Apache resistance leader, ca. 1874–86, hung over entry to main cell block.

Tears have fallen from my children's eyes
the hot salty taste of the white man's lies
their promise of our future, begins
with tales of our ancestors and their savage sins
how is it, we never seem to care
about our lives, and are we treated fair?
we're fools or they now call it wards
of the government, who supply us with rags and boards
to build our meager homes, with toilets in the kitchen
and clothes your children wore, and you say we're bitch'in?
well, for once white man, what you say is true
we're taking what is ours and there's nothing you can do!

Tears have fallen from my Mothers eyes
her years are leaving with soft good-byes
no more will she sleep with tired bones
her worries are over. We children are finding our homes
old eyes have seen all the things
like the disease and disaster that whitey brings
my Mother has seen what the "Beneficial Bureau" has done
like give us all those economic opportunities, which were none
you've tried your best to make our land white
by robbing us of our heritage and our birthrights
your attempts of suppression are through
we're taking what is ours and there's nothing you can do!

—Anonymous
San Francisco Public Library

7

Alcatraz, symbol of oppression, rock prison of liberation
        I come to take you into my possession
You possessed many braves full of indignation
        Against the oppressive system.

Yes, I come to change you into a symbol of redemption
        And to include you
Rock reservation of the melting pot, into a symbol of redemption
        And to include you
Rock reservation of the melting pot
        In the struggle of liberation

Oh, free territory of the Pacific
        you at one time were beautiful
But now you are covered with ugliness
        Stay on the side of the struggle
Or disappear into the deep water of the Pacific
        As my buffalo disappeared into the plains

Alcatraz, death buffalo of the sea
        I want to revive you that my children may ride you
Into the stampede of freedom and hope
        For their minds and bodies.

This time we fight not with bows and arrows
        But with pencils and books
Yes I want my children to be worthy of my grandfather Geronimo
        I want to teach them that he did not die in vain.

—Anonymous

We are here to stay, men, women, and children . . . . We are a proud people! We are Indians! We have observed and rejected much of what so-called civilization offers. We are Indians! We will preserve our traditions and ways of life by educating our own children. We are Indians! We will join hands in a unity never before put into practice. We are Indians! Our Earth Mother awaits our voices. We are Indians of All Tribes! WE HOLD THE ROCK!

—Indians of All Tribes

Coast Guard intercepts Indian people en route to Alcatraz Island.

THE WHITE MAN'S WAY

You gave us a treaty and took our land
And you stole our children away—
Our water turned bad, the wind blew sands
The white man had come to stay!

Then the corn gave out and the buffalo died
And our children slept alone,
Black were our faces, our women cried
And our young men started to roam!

The whiskey was cheap, the food was high
And our horses starved in the field.
For when people are beaten, people will die
And the fate of our tribes was sealed!

Our spirits were crippled as broken wings
The bright land turned to dust
You gave us the Bible and some old things
And ordered us to learn to trust!

Aii, we signed your treaty and burned our tent
And waited for promises to be kept.
We heard your words; we learned what they meant
Our brothers drank and our mothers wept!

But, today our young men from all of the tribes
Hold this place as Indian Land.
Take back your treaty, take back your bribes
On this Island, together we stand!

—Lonewolf, Blackfoot
December 2, 1969

ALCATRAZ VISIONS

Coast Guard boats circling the island,
Navy helicopters hovering like vultures
military American melting pot
with Liberty and Justice, they say.

Creatures of wonder are the children
as they run across the concrete fields,
young eaglets of an Indian tomorrow
children of all tribes, here on Alcatraz.

Government officials squirming,
red-eared at the sounds of a sucking child,
Alcatraz mother who must be there
for the words of her child's tomorrow.

Boatload of new arrivals,
Navajo, Sioux, Hoopa, Pomo,
spirit, heart, eyes and feet
testing the ground of unity.

San Francisco so close to us,
vertical fabrications erase the rounded hills,
bright lights and sounds and smells of decay,
drift to this turtle island.

Sunday sailboats clustered close,
snapping sails and wind and voices,
Tim studies this scene of white gaiety
and says, "Once, it was our people out there."

A warship pushes swiftly by,
a jet screams in mechanical rage;
when dugout and birchbark canoes glide,
rage is not the call of snow birds

Steel bridges all around this Bay,
connecting land in bumper to bumper pain,
dreams on Alcatraz are of a different bridge,
fashioned on sunlight and soft voices.

My father hunted the giant mammoth
and I am only five hundred years old,
who can still remember the blood of Montezuma
and the crying at Wounded Knee.

—Peter Blue Cloud

THE DRUMS OF ALCATRAZ

Down to the shore our people come
Following sounds of the Indian drum
For this is a day of victory —
Shoshone, Yakima, and Cree!

In our peoples' eyes, a new spirit gleams
The shining hope of old, old dreams
For we are proud of our young men
Pomo, Blood, and Algonquin!

Our children laugh and sing our song
The people dance all day long,
Around the Island our people walk
Blackfoot, Apache, and brave Mohawk!

Across the waters of the gleaming Bay
Our people come throughout the day
To laugh and dance the long night through
Paiute, Navajo, and Sioux!

O, my people, hear our drums
The drums of Alcatraz!

—Lonewolf, Blackfoot
December 1, 1969

We Hold the Rock

Indians of All Tribes greet our brothers and sisters of all races and tongues upon our Earth Mother. We here on Alcatraz Island, San Francisco Bay, California represent many tribes of the United States as well as Canada, Alaska, and Central and South America.

We are still holding the Island of Alcatraz in the true names of Freedom, Justice, and Equality, because you, our brothers and sisters of this earth, have lent support to our just cause. We reach out our hands and hearts and send spirit messages to each and every one of you. WE HOLD THE ROCK!

—Indians of All Tribes

WHITE MAN'S POISON

O, My lost young men
Return to home again.

You know of the smallpox blankets
And the loss of the buffalo.
And you know of the dead at Wounded Knee,
Where sweetgrass will not grow!

You know of hunger everywhere,
And sorrow cold as rain,
You know your father's broken lance,
You feel your mother's pain!

You know the tribes that are no more,
Who dance without a sound,
But you drank the white man's poison
And you passed his bottle round.

You know you lost your spirit
And threw away your pride,
And drank the white man's poison
And forgot your people died!

So leave the white man's ways
And chant old songs once more;
Come hang on the Sun Dance Pole
And feel your Spirit soar!

Put on your beaded shirt, my son,
And sing our Sacred Song
Your lodge can stand in a willow grove
So your spirit will be strong.

O, my proud young men
Do not forget again!

—Lonewolf, Blackfoot

THE INDIAN QUESTION

Why won't you give us the Island—
What is it that you fear?

Why don't you try to set things right
Now that we are here?

Why won't you give us our land and schools
And let us begin to build?

Are you ashamed of what you've done—
Of what you've spoiled and killed?

Why don't you give us Alcatraz,
What does it mean to you?

What if the Mohawk and Navajo
Join Cherokee and Sioux?

For we are one people, proud and strong
And we must have this land!

We'll build a new and sacred place
According to an Indian plan!

So do not fear, O, poor white man
We do not want your life!

We turn instead to our Indian Way
Free from your hate and strife!

—Lonewolf, Blackfoot
December 3, 1969

23

And I am only five hundred years old
and my dream is just now beginning,
as the drums of Alcatraz throb my spirit
and all the people do a round dance,

and our Earth Mother is a round dance
and all the stars circle our eagle drums,
and the children of Alcatraz run and play
and glad I am to be a youth of only five hundred years.

—Peter Blue Cloud

Indian occupiers meet in the warden's house on Alcatraz Island. Photo of Geronimo hangs over fireplace.

ALCATRAZ IS NOT AN ISLAND

We came to Alcatraz with an idea. We would unite our people and show the world that the Indian spirit would live forever. There was little hate or anger in our hearts, for the very thought of a lasting unity kept us who are in harmony with life. From this island would grow a movement which must surely encompass the world. All men of this earth must hunger for peace and fellowship . . . .

Alcatraz, the idea, lives. We can only pray the Great Spirit that all brothers and sisters who can understand our song join us. Speak now your love of the Indian people. Dance with us the great unity. Chant with us the earth renewal. Let all men and women be proud. Let our children bathe in truth and never know the broken promises of the past. Let Indians of All Tribes be the pathway to People of one earth.

—Indians of All Tribes

AN INDIAN'S SONG

Stand strong, my brothers on the Rock
Do not despair!

Be brave, my brothers on the Rock
Our spirits there!

Walk tall, my sisters on the Rock
Stand up with your men!

Grow fast, my children on the Rock
Learn our ways again!

O, Indians of Alcatraz
Lift up your eyes!

—Lonewolf, Blackfoot
December 4, 1969

THE WOMEN OF ALCATRAZ

A hai - A hai - A hai

Our women are brave on Alcatraz
They work like the hard North Wind

A hai - A hai - A hai

Our women are gentle on Alcatraz
They sway like the sweet South Wind

A hai - A hai - A hai

Our women are wise on Alcatraz
They sing like the fresh East Wind

A hai - A hai - A hai

Our women are loving on Alcatraz
They smile like the warm West Wind

O, women of Alcatraz!

—Lonewolf, Blackfoot
November 25, 1969

31

ALCATRAZ RAIN

Throughout the cold and winter nights
We tended to our fires,
We drew our blankets close around
And watched the waves crash higher.

Though the cold waves beat on Alcatraz,
Indian hearts are stout,
For white men think we'll go away—
But we'll live this winter out!

For the North Wind is our Brother;
We share his bitter shock;
Aii—we are the warriors of Alcatraz,
And we will hold the Rock!

—Lonewolf, Blackfoot

ALCATRAZ ISLAND

We feel that this so-called Alcatraz Island is more than suitable for an Indian reservation, as determined by the white man's own standards. By this we mean that this place resembles most Indian reservations in that:

1. It is isolated from modern facilities, and without adequate means of transportation.
2. It has no fresh running water.
3. It has inadequate sanitation facilities.
4. There are no oil or mineral rights.
5. There is no industry and so unemployment is very great.
6. There are no health care facilities.
7. The soil is rocky and non-productive; and the land does not support game.
8. There are no educational facilities.
9. The population has always exceeded the land base.
10. The population has always been held as prisoners and kept dependent upon others.

Further, it would be fitting and symbolic that ships from all over the world, entering the Golden Gate, would first see Indian land, and thus be reminded of the true history of this nation. This tiny island would be a symbol of the great lands once ruled by free and noble Indians.

—Indians of All Tribes

Don't feel you're a stranger here.
This is your land, this is my land.
This is Indian country.
My ancestors lived here; the Great Spirit put them here,
Just like he did the oak trees and the water.
Feel welcome. Let your spirit be free.

—Raymond Lego

Nature never discourages
"Come along,
            You belong
    here,
in harmony with me!"

I go and know that I am in
        the heart of life
        and love her
and she loves me

Each day in every way
        The magic of truth and love
        draw me to them and
        their unquenchable bosom

Great spirit help them and me
        to reach across and touch.

—Jerry Hill, Oneida
San Francisco Public Library

WHY YOU ARE HERE

What Earth Mother and Spirit Father
have given you,

You must develop
and return to the life

of which we all are part
and will return to.

—Jerry Hill, Oneida
San Francisco Public Library

The question has been asked—why did we choose to occupy an abandoned prison rather than a more desirable land location. The answers to that question are many. To we Indian people the answers are obvious. Alcatraz Island is a symbol of what we Indian people have today. It bears a remarkable resemblance to Indian reservation life, as neither have enough water, there are no natural resources and the government can't find any use for it. Thus Alcatraz became discarded land. We think it has more value than that of a discarded prison. The stigma that a convict must bear throughout his life is a burden we Indians are familiar with; bars and barbed wire are not our jailers as we are prisoners of inequality, discrimination, and social contempt and injustices . . . and that is where the Alcatraz symbolism is. Alcatraz was a prison, a symbol of what your society has produced!

—Indians of All Tribes

Richard Oakes, Mohawk student leader, second from right, oversees delivery of supplies to Alcatraz during Coast Guard blockade.

FIRST BROTHER

I bind the sinew tight
      arrow to foreshaft
feather to base
      power

swift deer, I dream your eyes
brother so fast, I drift upon a wind
our grandfather has touched us both
who fashions the mountain's climb

to approach that sacred spring
to sweat the body to sky
brother dear, you stand in wonder
      and my heart and finger bleed

I pull the bow tight
      arrow to sinew
my brother, I sing you forever
strength for my child.

—Peter Blue Cloud

45

Jennie Joe (Navajo) designed the Alcatraz flag. She became known as the Betsy Ross of Alcatraz.

THE ROCKS OF ALCATRAZ

The wild pony stomp of Crazy Horse
Thunders just over the hill
For brave men ride to fight and die
And defy the white man's will!

O, our fires burn bright
Throughout the night
On the rocks of Alcatraz!

The wild chant of Blackfeet men,
And the cries of their women, too,
Join with the songs of the Navajo
The Cherokee and Sioux!

O, our children play
In the Indian way
On the rocks of Alcatraz!

For we are the men who were wild and free
And now dawns our new day—
We Indians know, we Indians feel
The old brave Indian way!

For brave strong men
Lead us again
On the rocks of Alcatraz!

—Lonewolf, Blackfoot
November 27, 1969

47

ALCATRAZ

As lightning strikes the Golden Gate
and fire dances the city's streets,
a Navajo child whimpers the tide's pull
and Sioux and Cheyenne dance lowly on the ground.

Tomorrow is breathing my shadow's heart
and a tribe is an island, and a tribe is an island
and silhouettes are the Katchina dancers
of my beautiful people.

Heart and heaven and spirit
written in a drum's life cycle
and a tribe is an island, forever,
forever we have been an island.

As we sleep our dreaming in eagles,
a tribe is an island
and a tribe is a people—
in the eternity of Coyote's Mountain

—Peter Blue Cloud

49

Coast Guard boat, Red Power symbol, and burnt-out
skeleton of warden's house following fire on Alcatraz
Island, June 2, 1970.

COMMUNION

The rain falls
    In slow motion
    That I might see
each drop disappear
    beneath my feet

A thousand million
    of the myriad colors
Splashing in that
    inexorable current

How beautiful nature
    adapted each thing
    to its environmental
    existence.

As I am at once
    the lowest and
    greatest of
        the spirit of life

The demanding current
begs me go.
    The frightened say no
Till mind and spirit
    say relent
the dissipating fear is spent.

—Jerry Hill, Oneida
San Francisco Public Library

51

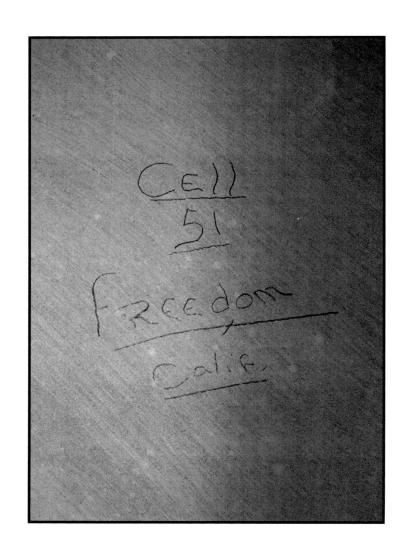

ALCATRAZ WINDS

Alcatraz winds barely speak
say not a word
too much said already
in singing storms on the mainland
decades past and a hive
unseen
honeybees of light; separate from
artery-heart of bigness and
dogbiscuit eyes flaking out
of vision—
can it be too little,
of no meaning and worth
only paper seawetted?
What is this song silent
throbbing over gray fog?

—Anonymous

THE RESERVATION

Oh hear my words, oh hear my cry
Red rock, sand and earth so dry

Daytime heat, a scorching hell
See my people, a walking shell
Nighttime cold, a great blue sphere
Bitter cold, as the hearts that put me here

I look in the sky, the stars I see are
Numbered wishes for my people and me
Babies born in this cruel land know
Not a world they'll understand

For when told of old use to be
What good are words to paint a tree?
When you are hot, when you thirst
My son, matters not—you were here first.

For your sin was not ignorance, but in
Believing his words even before they were taught to you

Oh hear my words, oh hear my cry
Red rock, sand and earth so dry

Is my only hope a liquid flame that burns my throat and steals my
name?
Is my only escape my woman's loom that tells my past and foretells
my doom?

Oh hear my words, Oh hear my cry
Red rock, sand and earth so dry

—Chris Lane, Cherokee

We dance the fog back to the ocean
and we dance the stars into being.
Our voices mock the whiteman's fog horn
and soon the fog horns are forgotten,
as are the lights of the surrounding cities.

We dance upon this turtle island, an isolated people from the rest of society.
An isolation long imposed upon us by a colonial system of government
which has never truly sought to understand us.

We dance on our turtle island and draw strength from one another
and from the past. Isolated, we will learn unity and learn to speak out our
    demands
to a deaf government.

We dance the stars in their sky passage and time does not exist.
The fire is a pile of embers with a small group still sitting around it
talking, talking.

We join the dance and feel the magic which is passing from hand to hand.
All tribes and unity are the words of the drum and all tribes in unity are the
dancers. The ancient dream of Indian unity is begun.

—Peter Blue Cloud, *Alcatraz Is Not an Island*

PROCLAMATION TO THE GREAT WHITE FATHER AND ALL HIS PEOPLE

We, the native Americans, reclaim the land known as Alcatraz Island in the name of all American Indians by right of discovery.

We wish to be fair and honorable in our dealings with the Caucasian inhabitants of this land, and hereby offer the following treaty:

We will purchase said Alcatraz Island for twenty-four dollars ($24) in glass beads and red cloth, a precedent set by the white man's purchase of a similar island about 300 years ago. We know that $24 in trade goods for these 16 acres is more than was paid when Manhattan Island was sold, but we know that land values have risen over the years. Our offer of $1.24 per acre is greater than the 47 cents per acre the white men are now paying the California Indians for their land.

We will give to the inhabitants of this island a portion of the land for their own to be held in trust by the American Indian Affairs and by the bureau of Caucasian Affairs to hold in perpetuity—for as long as the sun shall rise and the rivers go down to the sea. We will further guide the inhabitants in the proper way of living. We will offer them our religion, our education, our life-ways, in order to help them achieve our level of civilization and thus raise them and all their white brothers up from their savage and unhappy state. We offer this treaty in good faith and wish to be fair and honorable in our dealings with all white men.

—Indians of All Tribes

INSPIRATION

Bright, clear, green trees and
                              shrubs
And all the sounds of love

Nature, our mother earth,
                    harmonizes
and the will of the

                    Great Spirit
is set free

—Jerry Hill, Oneida
San Francisco Public Library

TOMORROW

We have wept the blood of countless ages
      as each of us raised high the lance of hate,
ours is the beauty of foreverness, if we but
      accept that which our Creator freely gives.
Now let us dry our tears and learn the dance
      and chant of the life cycle
tomorrow dances behind the sun in sacred promise
      of things to come for children not yet born,
for ours is the potential of truly lasting beauty
      born of hope and shaped by deed.
Now let us lay the lance of hate upon this soil.

—Peter Blue Cloud

Jim-Vaughn Linda-Aranaydo Ross-Hardin Burnell-Blindman Kay Many Horse John-Martell Rick-Evening John-Virgil

That defied the United States Armed Forces on Nov. 14, 1969 by taking Alcatraz-Island and returning it to the Rightful Owners —— the American - Indians.

"Indian-Joe" Morris

The Law of Our Father and Mother

Liquid images tell
They tell the story very well

Nuances of every nature
Are all the same in stature

Because the ambiguous answer
is a lie, is a truth, is a growth like cancer

The Infinitesimal things happen at once
and too enormous to conceive
So I sit alone this once
trying to believe

If there is a basic truth
One basic law that all
things must obey
It is the cycle of life:
things are born
things die
and we may not change it.

—Jerry Hill, Oneida
San Francisco Public Library

It was really a strange feeling to be going out to Alcatraz. When you got there they had slogans painted on the walls, "Red Power," "Welcome to All Indians," and lots of different signs painted all over the island in huge letters. It was weird. It was like going to a reservation in the middle of San Francisco Bay, because there were only Indians.

—Dan Bomberry
Doris Duke Oral History Project

They did it to bring public attention to the conditions of American Indians today. But once they got out there they realized that it was possible to use the island as an area independent of government control. There were a lot of very intelligent people who sat down and had council meetings, for awhile just about every day. They'd sit down and hash out the direction things were to go. It was pure and direct democracy in the truest form.

—Dan Bomberry
Doris Duke Oral History Project

The whole action of taking the island was symbolic of telling the American Government and American people that they are not going to continue to steal our lands nor are they going to tell us what to do. We are contradicting our whole move of liberation if we just wait for the Government. We are Indians who want action and we cannot let the Government continue to ignore us. We cannot let Alcatraz die because just as it was symbolic in reawakening Indian consciousness and bringing attention to the Indian people, it will be symbolic of our death if it should die . . . . We need title to have complete and permanent victory.

—LaNada Boyer, letter to Indians of All Tribes

It is difficult for most Americans to comprehend that there still exists a living community of nearly one million Indians in this country. For many people, Indians have become a species of movie actor periodically dis-patched to the Happy Hunting Grounds by John Wayne on the "Late, Late Show."

—*Vine Deloria,* New York Times Magazine, *March 8, 1970*

Indians regarded the capture of Alcatraz as the beginning of a new movement to recapture the continent and assert tribal independence from the United States, and it was finally this issue that Alcatraz came to symbolize.

—*Vine Deloria, Jr.,* Behind the Trail of Broken Treaties

73

Indians of All Tribes, who were we? From reservations and urban settlements, government boarding schools, street gangs or giant cities, plains, and desert, horse people, sheep herders, fishermen of the coastal rivers, hunters of the frozen north, we had come. Never before had the dream of Indian unity been put into reality in such a sudden way as at Alcatraz . . . .

—*Peter Blue Cloud, "Alcatraz Diary,"* Alcatraz Is Not an Island

An Old Indian's Thanksgiving Song

A - hai - hai - hai—

We who were quiet with apathy and despair
We who saw our mothers die and heard our fathers cry
We who have watched our land turn barren—
Today with pride, hold heads up high
Salute our young who bravely dare
Indian hopes to rise, Indian dreams realize!
Throughout this land our thankful song
Swells across the sky, and Indians cry
For land and bread and righting of the wrong!
    O, Indians of Alcatraz
You have made us men again!
Tall Blackhawk stands with Sitting Bull
Wise Tecumseh speaks with great Cochise
And all the tribes in all the lands
Send up the song for victory and peace
    O, brave young Indians
Your mothers weep no more!

—Lonewolf, Blackfoot

77

The walls of man
Soon too, will crumble
And time will see
What man has said.
That time will come.
. . . Stone over bone.

—Thunder Hawk
July 11, 1970

You are weary
and your steps grow
slower
you pray for strength
and you think of the
little ones
for them you fight and
for them you gave the
promise of freedom
and for them you will die
look ahead my brother
let the dream of liberty
sustain your spirit
and you will laugh at the
enemy once more
for your arrow is ready

—Lydia Yellowbird

The lamentations
of the loom
call the spirit to awaken
And I glimpse the last rays
of the beauty of the
setting sun
And I ride my horse
that has seen many battles
in full warrior's dress
to join my people
In the land where the
sun now sets
I am free, and I am at peace
with my spirit
My people call,
I will go to them.

—Lydia Yellowbird

When you came
you found a people
with red skin
they were one
with all living things
But you did not see this
beauty
instead you saw them
as animals, primitive
savage
Because you had lost this
whole
In the progress of your civilization
look now what your knowledge
has made them

—Lydia Yellowbird

THE ROCK OF OUR FOUNDATION:
MOTHER EARTH

We made that Rock ours, again
It was stolen, but now we claim it back

We dance that Rock into our hearts,
and sing the Spirit of the Land
into our Souls

The symbol of Alcatraz stands for
all Native people and all Native lands
stolen and abused

Alcatraz was desecrated and disrespected
left for dead

But the Native People danced and sang life back into
the Rock of our foundation:
Mother Earth

The layers and layers of concrete could not
stop the flowing of spirit between the Land
and her People

We danced the Spirit back into the Land

And now, there are only remains of the prison,
we see that man-made things cannot last

Flowers and green things still grow on Alcatraz
and seagulls have become her keepers, for a time

The rain gutters on the buildings
no longer shed the nourishing rain of Father Sky,

No, the gutters are now filled with Earth and grass
The life of Mother Earth is lifted up,
3 stories high, in praise to the sky

A mixing of life-giving-Spirit happens even in a rain gutter

Yes, we made Alcatraz ours again
We brought back our connection to that
"Sacred Rock"

Isn't it now time to heal all wounds of
Mother Earth and Her People?

Leavenworth, San Quentin, Corcran
Lompoc, Attica, and hundreds more
and
Let's not forget Pine Ridge, Rosebud, Klamath,
Fort Sill, Colville
AND HUNDREDS MORE

These places are ALL prisons
holding our People and our Mother

Now is a time for Freedom
This is why we Dance and Sing
and
Walk for Justice

We walk together,
on the Rock of our Foundation:
Mother Earth

—Cheryl Anne Payne (Bautnuq Punguk), Eskimo

BUFFALO SONG

Long ago, sweetgrass grew high
And green trees brushed a golden sky!

Long ago, brown beaver made a dam
And eagles clasp'd the mountain ram!

Long ago, the buffalo were there
With white tailed deer and grizzly bear!

    Ah hai — Ah hai — Ah hai!

Then white men plundered ov'r the land
Buffalo bled, red rivers ran!

Our brave men fought and then lay down
To die on that cold and bloody ground!

Our children ran, our women cried
The deer, the bear, the people died!

    Ah hai — Ah hai — Ah hai!

The hard years came, the sweetgrass went
And dust blew thistles for our tent!

Our young men drank, our women wailed
Our old men bowed, our children failed!

The land was bad, the water sour
A beaten people without power!

    Ah hai — Ah hai — Ah hai!

Then drums from Alcatraz were heard
Blown by the wind, borne by the bird!

Our young men stand brave and tall
And Alcatraz will never fall!

And once again, sweetgrasses grow
And once again, the bear, the buffalo!

Ah hai — Ah hai — Ah hai!

—Lonewolf, Blackfoot
November 30, 1969

89

ALCATRAZ MEDICINE

Wo hai — Wo hai — Wo hai!

Some fur, glass beads, a thong of hide
And the tips of an Eagle's wing—
Will make me a man again!

Wo hai — Wo hai — Wo hai!

Hot fire, strong meat, a ring of stone
And the smile of a Blackfoot girl
Will make me a man again!

Wo hai — Wo hai — Wo hai!

Brave men, strong wind, a bright red dawn
And my brothers on Alcatraz
Will make me a man again!

Wo hai — Wo hai — Wo hai!

Strong wind, dark night, the sound of waves
On the sacred rock of Alcatraz
Will make me a man again!

Wo hai — Wo hai — Wo hai!

Long years, barren land, the smell of death
All fade on the winds of Alcatraz
And make me a man again!

—Lonewolf, Blackfoot
November 29, 1969

91

A Vision

A free mind bears the will of the spirit.
        The child had reached to hit. A
Childish reaction to the rejection of its
selfishness. But the strong arm of
the parent gently laid a restraining
hand on the tiny raised arm. The
large arm was guided by the knowledge
and strength of truth.
        "No, child," in a voice at once
not spoken but understood in the
beautiful entirety of its meaning.
A moment of totality in communication
created itself.
        Thus the balm of truth passed
through the large gentle fingers
into the rigid small arm
and between their hearts.
        So the teacher accepted this vision
knowing he was part of one of the
fingers of the hand of the Spirit Father.

—Jerry Hill, Oneida
San Francisco Public Library

KEEPERS OF THE FLAME

I'll make my stand on Alcatraz
Tho it may be my last
Past souls are with me once again
'Tis the gathering of the past.

The broken bodies laid to waste
Upon the sands of time
'Tis like a mirror of myself
We cannot die this time.

We must make new the very old
And rekindle the spark of life
This stand I make is not alone
There are thousands in this strife.

There are millions who should walk
Once more in gallant liberty
Across the plains and o'er the hills
To keep the fires of freedom free.

Tributes to those who gave their all
And hope to us who keep the flame
A will to live with the guts to fight
To hold high forever the Indian name.

So each of us who stands alone
Stands not alone but together
Each one can do his mite or most
And we will stand forever.

Each one of you must hold the flame
O'er your head for all the world to see
Pick up the torch that was tossed to you
And walk again in Liberty.

To those of us who kept the flame
Out here alone on Alcatraz
We ask of you who really care
To be our strength on Alcatraz

So once again the world will know
Of proud people they could not kill
Then as a united army
We will walk beyond Alcatraz.

—Helen C. Becker, reprinted in *Akwesasne Notes*

MEDICINE MEN FROM THE LAND OF THE SUN

Out of the East they came
Up from the Land of the Sun—
      Petter Mitten with Medicines
      Petter Mitten with Prayer
      Mad Bear with Medicines
      Mad Bear with Prayer
the white man's medicines were weak
our Brother did not heal—
        Useless were the white man's instruments
        Empty were the white man's words.

A thousand years of wisdom
Carried three thousand miles—
      Holy Men of Medicine,
         come to prove to all again
         the weakness of the white man's way
Listen!
The white man laughed the laughter, the laughter of fools—
        fools who knew nothing of healing the Spirit
        fools who knew nothing of healing the Flesh,
      white men who listened only to the silent talk
      of their instruments, strangling the whispering of Hearts
until
      their minds could do no more, Despair came from their tongues
              Despair came from their eyes!

Then came the Indian Holy Men
With prayers to heal the ailing Heart of our Brother
With medicines to please the Healing Spirits
              strong medicines for a strong man!
Oh white man, weak man, why do you listen only to your playthings,
        is your heart so dead?
You forget the Healing Spirits, perhaps you never knew them—
        will you ever learn?

Poor, poor white man, the walls of your building still ring with
                                        your hollow laughter—
    your eyes have seen the power of olde ways
                                        but you will not see!

White man listen!
                Our Brother lives!
                Our Brother Heals,
                    Indian Medicine is strong
                    will you now believe?
                The proof lies healing before your disbelieving eyes,
                    Look!
                        perhaps this time you will see
                                with open eyes
                                        the Truth.

                —Csi-mu Mup-pah, Pit River Indian Nation

97

If we gather together as brothers and come to a common agreement, we feel that we can be much more effective . . . . So we must start somewhere. We feel that if we are going to succeed, we must hold on to the old ways. This is the first and most important reason we went to Alcatraz Island.

—*Indians of All Tribes*
December 6, 1969

Our parents were forbidden to speak their own language, or dance their own dances, and they were pushed into government boarding schools that were trying to teach them how to be "civilized," which meant losing their own identity . . . . Since the Civil Rights law, they've only taken down the signs that say "No Dogs and Indians Allowed."

—*Indians of All Tribes*

Before we took Alcatraz, people in San Francisco didn't even know that Indians were alive.

—*Indians of All Tribes*

We needed attention brought to our people, and we needed a place to get together in the City so that we didn't become victims of assimilation.

—*Indians of All Tribes*

Our anger at the many injustices forced upon us since the first white man landed on these sacred shores has been transformed into a hope that we be allowed the long-suppressed right of all men to plan and to live their own lives in harmony and cooperation with all fellow creatures and with Nature.

—*Indians of All Tribes*

We came to Alcatraz with an idea. We would unite our people and show the world that the Indian spirit would live forever. There was little hate or anger in our hearts, for the very thought of a lasting unity kept us whole and in harmony with life. From this island would grow a movement which must surely encompass the world. All men of this earth must hunger for peace and fellowship.

The idea was born and spread across this land, not as a fire of anger, but as a warming glow.

Alcatraz was born a mountain, surrounded by the waters of a great salt sea. By hands of hate was this island transformed into a symbol of fear and oppression. For too short a time this same island was held in trust by Indians of All Tribes, who sang its praise as a part of mother earth, and who cleansed the evil with the sacred tobacco.

Alcatraz is again the hateful symbol of oppression. Our Indian people have been removed from sacred ground, our children have felt guns at their heads. Steel fences are again being put up. All approaches to the island are being guarded and patrolled. Armed with weapons of war and the sterile theories of law, they try desperately to keep out the Indian spirit. We send out our voices to that desolate rock, and are gifted with echoes which resound our strength.

Alcatraz, the idea, lives. We can only pray the Great Spirit that all brothers and sisters who can understand our song join us. Speak now your love of the Indian people. Dance with us the great unity. Chant with us the earth renewal. Let all men and women be proud. Let our children bathe in truth and never know the broken promises of the past. Let Indians of All Tribes be the pathway to People of one Earth.

—*Indians of All Tribes*

We came to Alcatraz because we were sick and tired of being pushed around, exploited, and degraded everywhere we turned in our own country. We selected Alcatraz because it is a place of our own . . . .

We can beat our drums all night long if we want to and not be bothered or harassed by non-Indians and police. We can worship, we can sing, and we can make plans for our lives and the future of our Indian people and Alcatraz.

—Indians of All Tribes

Richard Oakes (Mohawk).

There was one old man who came on the island. He must have been eighty or ninety years old. When he stepped up onto the dock, he was overjoyed. He stood there for a minute and then said, "At last I am free!"

—Richard Oakes, Ramparts

Alcatraz was a place where thousands of people had been imprisoned, some of them Indians. We sensed the spirits of the prisoners. At times it was spooky, but mostly the spirit of mercy was in the air. The spirits were free. They mingled with the spirits of the Indians that came on the island and hoped for a better future.

—Richard Oakes, Ramparts

It was there [at San Francisco State] that one of the older people said, "All you young people, listen: We have been looking forward to this day when there would be something for you to do. You are our leaders."

—Richard Oakes, California History *(Spring 1983)*

Before dawn on November 10, 1969, they [the UCLA students] were on a boat to Alcatraz, where "this time we planned to stay."

—Richard Oakes, California History *(Spring 1983)*

Alcatraz is not an island. Alcatraz is not only here on the island, but it's part of every reservation, it's a part of every person.

—Richard Oakes

. . . this is actually a move, not so much to liberate the island, but to liberate ourselves for the sake of cultural survival . . . .

—Richard Oakes

I'd never heard anyone actually tell the world that we needed somebody to pay attention to our treaty rights, that our people had given up an entire continent, and many lives, in return for basic services like health care and education, but nobody was honoring those agreements. For the first time, people were saying things I felt but hadn't known how to articulate. It was very liberating.

—Wilma Mankiller, Parade, August 18, 1991

When Alcatraz occurred, I became aware of what needed to be done to let the rest of the world know that Indians had rights too. Alcatraz articulated my own feelings about being an Indian. It was a benchmark. After that, I became involved.

—Wilma Mankiller, Sacramento Bee, December 7, 1993

The torch of protest and change was grasped by Native Americans. In 1969, the rage that helped to give a voice and spirit to other minority groups spread through native people like a springtime prairie fire. And just as the tall grass thrives and new life bursts forth after the passage of those indispensable flames, we too were given a renewal of energy and purpose.

For my people and other native people whom we befriended in San Francisco, the federal termination and relocation programs dating from the 1950s had failed.

Then something happened that gave me the focus I was searching for. It all started in November of 1969, when a group of Native Americans representing more than twenty tribes seized a deserted island in the midst of San Francisco's glittering bay . . . . [T]hey took over the twelve-acre island to attract attention to the government's gross mistreatment of generations of native people. They did it to remind the whites that the land was ours before it was theirs . . . . The name of the island is Alcatraz. It changed my life forever.

—Wilma Mankiller, Mankiller

105

John Trudell, "the voice of Alcatraz," kept the nation aware of the Alcatraz occupation over "Radio Free Alcatraz."

It is often very hard being a revolutionary and the time is very consuming.

—John Trudell, "Radio Free Alcatraz"

The government's proposal is nothing more than the formation of another park, whether it be state or federally owned, unneeded, undesired, and actually an attempt to end the Alcatraz movement; the movement which is the hope of Indian people to advance themselves culturally and spiritually. A true belief of our own ideals . . . . We will no longer be museum pieces, tourist attractions, and politicians' playthings. We do not need statues to our dead because our dead never die—they are always here with us . . . . There will be no park on this island because it changes the whole meaning of what we are here for. We are tired and we are very sad. . . . We do not think that it is right to play politics with human individuals, the lives of people. We do not understand it, we do not like it, we will not be a part of it. We will work for the betterment of all people. . . . We have kept our word to the American people. Ours is a non-violent movement. We have made every effort to cooperate with the U.S. government. We have worked with them, met with them, and listened to them. We have done what they have asked up to this point, and not once have they voluntarily shown that they are willing to do the same for us. Our answer to the U.S. government that this island be turned into a park . . . our answer at this time and any other time is an emphatic NO!

—John Trudell, "Radio Free Alcatraz"

As long as we are out here there is no social worker, no BIA person going to tell us we are unfit for our children and take our children away from us and send them to a school, or whatever it is. They can't do that out here.

—John Trudell, "Radio Free Alcatraz"

Poverty is a state of mind, you know. You are as poor as you want to be. It comes down to, well we are poor in materialism, here I would say we are rich in Spiritualism. The outside society is rich in materialism, they've got no spiritualism at all . . . .

—John Trudell, "Radio Free Alcatraz"

This tiny island represents freedom for all Indian people living in the Americas, known as Canada, the United States, Mexico, and South America. These are all our great lands of Indian people now held in bondage by alien governments . . . . Our fight for this island representing freedom for all Indian people is non-violent. We came to this island unarmed, prepared to give our lives if necessary.

—John Trudell, "Radio Free Alcatraz"

Alcatraz is the beginning of the return of the Buffalo which means the coming back of our people, the return of the spirit. Alcatraz is a traditionalist spiritual movement. This is our prophecy and the Great Spirit is working for the people.

—John Trudell, "Radio Free Alcatraz"

We would like to see a strong sense of nationalism built and I think Alcatraz is starting to do that. Alcatraz started doing that just by the physical occupation and the followup like Pit River and the attention that has been put on the Taos people trying to get their land back and Blue Lake. The attention that has been put out on Washington fishing rights . . . . I see the Indian unity coming and that's what our whole objective is now. Whatever we do, we do for Indian people . . . . We don't want just the small battle, we are shooting for the overall victory and in the process of doing so this hasn't changed from the beginning to now.

—John Trudell, "Radio Free Alcatraz"

We won't deal with the government, it's just as simple as that. We are tired of being lied to and about. Now if the government wants to sit down and talk about serious issues, what we want to talk about, and they send someone with a little authority to deal, then maybe we'll sit down and talk.

—John Trudell, "Radio Free Alcatraz"

Alcatraz is a symbol all of America can identify with—all of America has heard of Alcatraz and by us taking this land we are taking something that the public is aware of being there, the former federal prison. By doing this it makes it possible for us to bring the spotlight on Indian problems in America, to know that all is not well with Indians in America. There are many people in the United States that are not even aware of how Indian people have to live and by taking Alcatraz I believe we are beginning to bring this awareness to these people . . . . Once the government has done what they very freely pleased to do with our lands and with the people, and the public has not been aware of what has been going on . . . . We are in the process of overcoming many years of Indian people not working together. But we are proving on this island, that it can be done . . . . We are getting stronger as each day goes by.

—John Trudell, "Radio Free Alcatraz," January 20, 1970

We are protesting, which according to the constitution of the United States, the people have the right to do. We are protesting injustices that have been directed toward us and this is what we get. They do not come out and shoot us . . . . Right now the government has a policy of not doing anything to upset the American people. They don't want to rock the boat, so they are not going to come in right now and rip us off the island because they don't want to rock to boat. The American people would get upset if the government would come in and arrest us. But they don't get upset by the fact that we don't have water out here. They don't get upset over the fact that it is unsanitary out here without water, that we can't keep the places as clean and healthy as they should be, and we

*would like them to be. We're out here and we've got things like fire haz-
ards; there's no water out here to put out things like fires. The water that
we do get in is brought in small containers and if anything bad ever
happens there's not much defense we have against it right now; but then
it's not my conscience.*

—John Trudell, "Radio Free Alcatraz"

*You go down 16th Street and see the Indian bars and see the people
that are drunk, and relocation has done nothing for them, cause you just
can't take a people and keep them uneducated and give them nothing—
for example, most of their early life, and just send them to a city and say
here, here is a job doing this and then cut you loose. I think I would just
as soon stay on the reservation, and be poor as to move to a city on relocation and have to live in a ghetto area, and that is exactly where they put us.*

—John Trudell, American Indian Historical Research Project

*We want to be free, we want the right to live like free men, as a free
people . . . . I'm asking for a chance to get a job, live where I want . . . .
I'm not trying to live next door to the great man you know. I just want a
chance. I don't think it is asking for too much.*

—John Trudell, "Radio Free Alcatraz"

Alcatraz is an idea—There is much symbolism here . . . .

—John Trudell, "Radio Free Alcatraz"

*[T]hey [the government] say they are going to make a park out of it and
it is going to have an Indian flavor. Yea, what's an Indian flavor? It means an
Indian's got to get burned I guess.*

—John Trudell, "Radio Free Alcatraz"

What we are asking for, what we are saying is that we want self-determination . . . .

—John Trudell, "Radio Free Alcatraz"

Indian patience and endurance being exhausted, we can not and will not wait any longer. From the facts, the logic and the varieties we have decided that it flows that we must and we do declare our land is ours again. As a first step we announce on behalf of all the Indian people that from this day forward we will exercise dominion and all rights of use and possession over Alcatraz Island in San Francisco Bay . . . . What we have done by this declaration, we have done for Indians, but to those whites who desire that their government be a government of law, justice, and morality, we say we have done it also for you. Signed Indians of All Tribes

—John Trudell, "Radio Free Alcatraz"

You have divided us by lines geographically, you have put us in urban areas, you have disbanded us, terminated us, starved us, killed us, but we are here, everyone of us are here. In our religion there is no ending for us. We are children of nature and we go back to nature. So our people still exist here, every blade of grass and every tree that grows is a part of us. We will not permit this genocide. If it takes violence it will come from the white man. It will not come from us. Here on Alcatraz we intend to stay because this genocide will stop with Alcatraz. From this day forward there is no place for the Indian to go but forward. He has been held back long enough.

—Stella Leach, "Radio Free Alcatraz"

Alcatraz is a start, it is a catalyst. Alcatraz is in the hearts and minds of all the Indian people, young or old.

—John Trudell, "Radio Free Alcatraz"

Since 1492 to the present, November 9th, 1969, the Indian people have been held in bondage. Alcatraz is a release from that bondage . . . .

—John Trudell, "Radio Free Alcatraz"

The most important thing the people of this country can do for Indian people is when they do these things, act out of sincerity, not out of politics, because politics, the way this society runs its political system, politics just don't work.

—John Trudell, "Radio Free Alcatraz"

Well, the general feeling of the people on the island—we want to see results. We don't want to hear words and we don't want to hear President Nixon talking to the white public. We want to hear him talking to Indians. When he is going to be talking about Indian issues and Indian affairs, we want the talk to be to us. We want to see results, positive results that affect Indian people, and not a lot of rhetoric. Deal with us and not the public because we are the ones that are directly involved in this.

—John Trudell, "Radio Free Alcatraz"

We know from 500 years of experience that the American Indian must stand before the world and the world courts alone . . . to correct all wrongs or the government will not stand rightly for us. The government of the United States constantly elects to ignore Indians. This practice must end!

—John Trudell, "Radio Free Alcatraz"

We the American Indians are god's children and created equal, have minds of our own, dignity, self-respect, loyalty, we look up to no man, look down on no man, and demand the same from all men.

—John Trudell, "Radio Free Alcatraz"

We are going to be applying for foreign aid shortly. I guess we are going to have to turn and ask other governments to do what the U.S. government should be doing but neglects to do.

—John Trudell, "Radio Free Alcatraz"

The isolation, that is what I like about it . . . . I mean it is obvious the white people can't come here . . . because an island you can keep it more separate than you can a reservation . . . .

—*Stella Leach*
American Indian Historical Research Project
University of New Mexico

When we come to Alcatraz . . . all of our troubles are left there on the dock . . . because out here we are just Indians and we don't have trouble with each other.

—*Stella Leach*
American Indian Historical Research Project
University of New Mexico

The occupants scrambled ashore, aware of their long journey and the new world that their landing will usher in. Their determined first steps to the higher land and rocks will end the old order and ultimately change their world forever.

—George P. Horse Capture, Seeds of Change *by Herman J. Viola and Carolyn Margolis*

Now, as I look back at these enlightening times, starting with Alcatraz . . . my gratitude is without measure. For no longer is our history locked away in isolation. Today we are familiar with our past, and it fills us with pride and stabilizes our journey into the future.

—George P. Horse Capture, Seeds of Change *by Herman J. Viola and Carolyn Margolis*

Alcatraz has served a number of purposes; it has served as an awakening to the general public and the world of the many injustices done to the American Indian in both the past and present. It has shown that we are proud of our culture and heritage and wish to retain it. It has shown that we can organize and develop unity. It has forced the federal government to recognize the problems facing the Indian community in the Bay Area to the extent of making funds available.

—Earl Livermore
Doris Duke Oral History Project

"Alcatraz was the Catalyst," she says, *"and the most important event in the Indian movement to date. It made me put my furniture in storage and spend my life savings."*

—*Grace Thorpe, daughter of Jim Thorpe*
Indian Voice *by Dean Chavers*

Federal marshals arrived on June 10, 1971 to remove Indian occupiers from Alcatraz.

. . . it's really not that obvious, except for the movements that went on out west, California, Washington, and all along there. The important thing is that these movements did happen because of Alcatraz.

—Ross Harden
Doris Duke Oral History Project

The federal marshals did ride on the Coast Guard boats when they had their blockade on the island, but they weren't successful. Every time someone came and threw supplies on our barge the Coast Guard cutter would chase them around the island and while they were gone, a couple more boats would dock next to our barge and give us more supplies, like food, water, pots, pans, etc. The blockade was lifted after two weeks.

—Ross Harden
Doris Duke Oral History Project

Well, militant is the way we took Alcatraz, not caring what anyone said or thought about it. It's putting out facts and not caring who tried to get in your way, and not caring how you go about doing it. Indians can demand things that they had a right to.

—Ross Harden
Doris Duke Oral History Project

When I speak of the movement, I mean Alcatraz, and the awakening of Indians . . . . But the most important thing in our minds was the fact that the Indians were getting stepped on and we wanted to make them aware of this. Someone came up with Alcatraz Island.

—Ross Harden
Doris Duke Oral History Project

ALCATRAZ . . . LIVES!!

You say they've gone????
All taken off . . .
all pushed off . . .
all pulled off . . .
all ripped off . . .
You say they've gone????

Listen then, listen long—
Hear that laughter . . .
Hear that cry . . .
Hear that child . . .
Hear that prayer . . .
Listen then, listen long—
The winds carry their songs.
The sun carries their warmth
The winds carry their songs.
The grass whispers their words.
You say they've gone????
Listen . . . whiteman . . .
Listen long.

—HaiHai PaWo PaWo, *Akwesasne Notes* (June 1971)

Federal marshals stand guard during removal of Indians from Alcatraz Island.

ALCATRAZ ARROW

A million acts of aggression
to a hardened heart seems few
It really doesn't concern us now.
those tribes

Driven by desperation
To follow their Indian star
They landed and held a rocky,
barren prison

An arrow was launched in protest
of the peering, staring, endless
eyes.

A small act of aggression
Small in view of the millions that
died—Indians

Huge act of aggression now
the government must act
every act against the Indian
uncounted

One small act must be requited.
Will there ever be justice
for the Indian?

—A. Kelsey

The Lord Giveth and the Whiteman Taketh Away.

—Anonymous, graffiti on Alcatraz

Richard Oakes and daughter Yvonne.

Yvonne Oakes, twelve-year-old daughter of Anne Oakes and step-daughter of Richard Oakes, was seriously injured on January 3, 1970, when she fell three stories in an abandoned apartment building on Alcatraz Island. On January 8, 1970, Yvonne passed away. The following poem was written in her honor.

FOR YVONNE

We have mourned the passing of a girl
and the drums have cleared the rainbow path
and our voices have praised the wheeling sun,
day into dark night into brighter day.

We hold hands in a circle unbroken
as eternal shadows dance foreverness
a girl, a child, a sister, a song—
we have wept the earth a sorrow

     a feather,
     a flower,
     a hand,
     a people.

—Anonymous

WHEN'S THE LAST BOAT TO ALCATRAZ
(FOR RICHARD OAKES)

When's the last boat to Alcatraz?
    I hear the foghorns and lonely gulls.
Who's skipper on that leaky tub,
    the Broken Treaty.
and what people drum and chant
    upon that turtle now?

It grows darker here, within this forest.
    They try to tell me that my brother died.
I laugh and my laughter echoes,
    through these redwoods
    breaking inner light.
I laugh and laugh and hear a pistol shot,
which is a loose rock falling from
    the cliff on Alcatraz.

A lone bear walks the wooded mountains
    of Pomo country, of Pit River country.
A tall bear, whose anger is a sometimes
    earthquake
    of gentle thunder.

When's the last treaty being written?

It is ten seconds to America, 1976.

It grows darker still as the sky eagle
folds those great winds
    upon my brother's sleep.
It is winter and the glaciers descend
    upon the cities
the harbors freeze over and the tug
boat "Good Citizen" is trapped
    between Alcatraz and myth.

132

It is cold and even the temperature
        of memory
            slows its course.

The breath of that lone bear
        is snuffing loudly
            among the giant redwoods.

When's the last boat to Alcatraz?
        (It was so cold and damp,
so little food,
        the children's laughter.
That fog we remember, out there.
        We played shadow games.
Close to fire's heat the drum's taut need,
        and our need
            a warmth of dancing.)

Such strange visions upon that rock.
        Hey, yes,
                these are tears
                    at last.

Told never to say that name again, and
told to dream of other islands
        dreaming instead
            of a bear,
                not lonely, but
dancing slowly and heavily.

My brother, Stands Tall, his name,
        now we wish his journey
            be in peace.

—Peter Blue Cloud
December 1972

ILLUSTRATIONS